A Daisychain

by Hetty Staples

Designed and published by JayT Ltd

Jackie Pullen: create@jayt.co.uk

I would like to dedicate this little book to my granddaughter Juliet, whom I dearly love. May she 'neverstopexploring'.

ISBN 978-0-9934968-0-6

Printed by Azimuth Print Ltd
Unit 2a, Princess Street, Bedminster, Bristol BS3 4AG

Contents

Preface 1
The house where I grew up 2
The party 6
Olive's morning adventure 7
Viking Dublin 8
Reaching the summit 9
A family picnic 10
Our cottage in Carraroe 12
Over the wall 15
Escape 16
Lament for Connemara 17
The unexpected find 18
A memoir 19
My native river 22
Dreaming of days gone by 24
Favourite trees 27
Running free 29
What lies down that path? 30
Murder in the glen 32
Ripples around Louis Macniece 34
The meeting place 36
Family album 37
Oakshott 38
The reunion 40
A Currabinny holiday 42
Little Stodham House 44
Is there a God? 46
On impulse 47
A significant building 48
A red letter day 50
What I see from where I stand 52
A walk in Montacute gardens 53
Loose living 54
A decade of continental holidays 55
Mobile phones 56
Time and tide wait for no man 57
Our South Downs town 58
The great sale 59
The queen bee 60

Index of Illustrations

Front Cover: *Pattern of daisies from a drawing by Hetty's grandmother*
Frontispiece: *Hetty's grand-daughter, Juliet Smith, in Florence*
Preface: *Hetty at the house in Stillorgan, Co Dublin*
Page 2 *Cappagh House*
Page 3 *Austrian Refugees at Cappagh*
Page 4 *Hetty's father with Tom Murray the ploughman*
Page 5 *A watercolour of Cappagh House (Hetty in the library window)*
Page 7 *Olive Howe (nee Denroche) as a child*
Page 11 *A family picnic with George Blueu*
Page 12 *The coast at Rossaveal (Connemara)*
Page 13 *The family cottage at Barraderry (Connemara)*
Page 15 *Donkey cart with Barclay Griffin*
Page 17 *Curragh at Carraroe*
Page 19 *Uncle Bob and Aunt Sis (Atkinson)*
Page 20 *Hetty's mother as a child*
Page 21 *Hetty with her grandmother and grandfather who is having his hair cut by John Power (inset Hetty with her parents)*
Page 23 *Bathing party in the River Blackwater at Lismore*
Page 25 *Hetty with Edith Frost in Wallingford*
Page 26 *Golden acacia at Little Stodham House*
Page 28 *Market Square, Petersfield*
Page 30 *Stepping Stones at Lough Dan, Co. Wicklow*
Page 31 *Boathouse at Lough Dan (inset Hetty with her daughters)*
Page 34-35 *At the races in Wincanton with John and Leila Rawlings*
Page 37 *Top: Jackie with her grandparents at Dublin Zoo.*
Below: Emily at Glen Cottage with her 11+ results
Pages 38-39 *Oakshott (at Hawkley). Mrs Field's house*
Page 41 *Hugh, Yvonne and her husband with Hetty at their house in Dublin*
Pages 42-43 *Angela Lorimer's house, Currabinny, Co. Cork*
Pages 44-45 *Little Stodham House, Liss*
Page 46 *Gerry and his initials in snowdrops at Little Stodham House*
Page 47 *At Petersfield Lake*
Page 49 *Watts Gallery. Sunflowers on screen*
Page 50 *Hetty reading*
Page 51 *Jonathan and Hetty*
Pages 52-53 *Montacute House, Somerset*
Page 58 *The Save the Children Sale, Petersfield (© Tracey Howe)*
Page 59 *Collage of Petersfield*
Back Cover: *A paper silhouette of Hetty (made in Montmartre, Paris)*

Preface

This is not an autobiography but rather a collection of memories; a pot au feu of my life in prose and poetry. They are the things that have stood the test of time sufficiently to record for my family in later years.

Its existence is chiefly due to the encouragement and secretarial skills of my partner, Jonathan Bennett, who has kept me focussed and put in many hours at the computer. He is himself a published author and has led me along the straight and narrow path of good grammar and metre wherever possible! I hope the result has been worth his while.

I have also enjoyed the help and support of two Writers' Circles. The one I inaugurated was for our local U3A Branch in Petersfield in 2003. The other was the East Hampshire Writers. I should also mention the Farnham Writers Circle (which features in my text entitled "A Red Letter Day").

My grandmother wrote a social history of our corner of south-east Ireland, which my elder daughter, Emily, has painstakingly reconstructed from its original flimsy manuscript and put in order for me. My younger daughter, Jackie, has taken on the task of editing and publishing this slim volume of memoirs. She has taken the cover design from a pattern of my grandmother's for a leather book cover. My father, Arland Ussher, was both a writer and an Irish scholar, so perhaps it is in the blood!

In any case, I am very grateful to all of the above for ensuring that when I have in due course to "make other arrangements", I may not be entirely forgotten.

As Robert Graves put it, "Blow on a dead man's embers and a live flame will start….."

The house where I grew up

My family, the Usshers, had lived in County Waterford since Adam and Eve! We were more "liberal" than most Anglo-Irish families. Cappagh, the house in which I grew up was just emerging from a turbulent epoch by the time I came along. Built for my great-grandparents in 1877, it replaced an earlier manor-house adjoining the stable-yard and, before that, a fortified tower-house.

My great-grandfather was a well-known ornithologist and founder-member of the Irish Society for the Protection of Birds. His collection of birds eggs sat in its cabinet in the Morning Room and is now in the National Museum in Dublin. He was also an archaeologist and the first person to discover the bones of mammoth and sabre-toothed tiger in a local cave.

Later on, my grandfather, Beverley Grant Ussher, became a School Inspector in England where he met and married my grandmother, Emily Jebb. She was the eldest of six Jebb siblings among whom figured Eglantyne and Dorothy, co-founders of Save the Children.

My mother came to Cappagh House as companion help and stayed to marry the only son, Percy Arland. He was an Irish scholar, a man of letters and a pacifist. Farming was not to his taste, yet during the "troubles" and the General Strike of the 1920's he learned to milk a cow! The house became a centre of much activity. In 1923, the IRA used it as a barracks and later the Black and Tans threatened it. A bullet hole remains to this day in the plate glass window of the front porch. However, because of the family's liberal views, the house was spared the fate of being fired as happened to so many of its neighbours.

My parents were married in 1925 and I was born a year later. I grew up virtually an only child as my brother was hydrocephalic and died young.

My grandmother founded the local branch of the Irish Countrywomen's Association and held classes in Cappagh House, teaching lace-making, leatherwork and cookery to the local farmers' wives. They manned stalls at the shows in Dungarvan, our shopping town. She also opened a local co-operative store and I was allowed to fill bags of sugar and rice, propped on a stool.

Every Christmas, we ran a party in the basement for the local children and I had to recite a poem in Irish. The bow window in the Drawing Room had a window seat which was a favourite haunt of mine for reading or painting. There was also a weeping elm on the terrace where I used to play "house" with my toys. A French window opened onto this terrace and much life was played out there. We had one tiny bathroom at the top of the back stairs. The paint was dark green and sticky because my grandmother saved the dregs of paint and forgot to add thinners. Consequently, you had to "peel" your towel off the window sill!

During the early part of the Second World War, some Austrian refugees came to live in a house on the estate to help with the farm work. They were lovely people and added much lively conversation to the place. They worked hard and kept cheerful in spite of their menial tasks, which was not what life should have held for them. Life on the farm occupied me as I rode on the hay rakes or churned

4

butter in the dairy. We took trips in the pony and trap but I never took to riding with the West Waterford Hounds; I was too young to enjoy the Hunt Balls. However, I learned to fish in the Lake and enjoyed the birds and red squirrels in the woods. The Blackwater Valley is very beautiful.

We sold the house in 1944. The family who bought it are still there now. During a visit to the house a year ago, I was cheered to see how Cappagh now has young life and been modernised. Gone is the basement kitchen with its black-leaded range and its cockroaches. The old dining room has been converted into a modern farm-house kitchen with Aga, dogs and all, while the front porch is full of welly-boots and footballs!

Much of the land has been sold off but the present owner has three sons who all have a foothold. The eldest lives in the house itself while his father has built a bungalow on the nearby hillside. The gatehouse and the dairy have been remodelled as holiday homes for the younger sons.

My beloved Cappagh House has survived the tumultuous decades of Irish politics. It still stands today, tranquil and at peace, as a monument to all that has gone before.

The party

Our family home, when I was growing up, was an imposing Victorian pile in Co. Waterford, Ireland. It was essentially a farm, with a walled-in farm yard and a big bell to call the men to work in the mornings. Their families lived in "tied" cottages on the estate, some of which were pretty basic. Barefoot children ran to school and fed the chickens. The older ones would drive a cart or help to put the hay in stacks.

My father was an Irish scholar and interested in preserving the mother tongue for future generations. Not so much the study of all subjects in Irish for Civil Service exams – a rather batty notion which held the country back – but rather in preserving the old myths, legends and country tales as told by the Shanachee around the fire. To this end he would follow the ploughman up and down the furrows, notebook in hand, as he drove his team of horses across the fields. He produced two volumes of stories in Irish which I'm ashamed to say I've never been able to read and neither have the majority of Irish citizens! He wanted to compile a taped library with the old story-tellers telling the tales but sadly it never happened.

Every year at Christmas time we would hold a party for the farm-workers' children. They were expected to bring along a recitation in Irish and there were prizes for the best performances – a doll or train engine or a chocolate Santa. I was expected to perform as well but was not allowed a prize, and probably never deserved one! The party was held in the old laundry-room in the basement. Mangle, wash-boards and clothes-horses were pushed to one side and a magic lantern installed. It ran on paraffin oil and smoked horribly but it projected sepia images on a screen - circus clowns, horses, roundabouts and swings, beach scenes and sailing boats. A far cry from computer games, but watched avidly in those far-off days.

Then we would all sit down at trestle tables to a party tea. There was a trifle with "hundreds and thousands" and buns with Smarties which my cousin Olive and I had decorated the day before. My uncle would dress up as Santa Claus and hand out the prizes and the take-home bags of sweets, all laboriously tied with ribbons and counted meticulously by Olive and me. We also helped to tie up the balloons and put out the crackers.

It was all very feudal but I like to think that those children enjoyed, in many ways, a freer, fuller early life than many of their modern counterparts.

Olive's morning adventure

There was once a little girl called Olive Denroche. She used to wake up just as the light began, and listen to the birds singing. First she heard the skylark, then she heard all these together: the swallows, swifts, house-martins, chiff-chaffs, whitethroats, willow wrens, flycatchers, grasshopper-warblers and nightjars.

She often wondered what the flowers were doing, and at last, one morning, before anybody was awake, she stole out of bed and went on her tiptoes to the back door.

She stole into the garden just in time to see the flowers open their petals. The daisies were the first to open with the sun; then all the others followed. Their names were polyanthuses, forget-me-nots, and wallflowers. Then she went round to the waste-ground to see what she would find there. She found dandelions in dozens, and celandines, but they had not opened because the sun had not come round that way yet.

Just as Olive was enjoying her adventure, her Nannie caught her. "My goodness, you *are* cold! Come into bed at once," she said, and put her to bed.

Olive was so cosy that she fell fast asleep. She dreamt that the flowers had turned into fairies and were dancing round her.

Written by Hetty Owen Ussher, aged 8

Viking Dublin

A thousand years ago every Dublin family had a home and a plot of its own. So runs the blurb accompanying a map of the probable configuration of Fishamble Street. This ancient part of the city has been extensively excavated and rebuilt in recent years and now resembles Covent Garden in its ambience. Fishamble was the site of the Shambles in the original Pool of Dublin or Dubh Linn. It was also the dwelling place of my first known ancestor in the 1480's. His name was Arlantor Uscher and he was a merchant, who gave his name to the adjoining quayside on the bank of the River Liffey close by Christchurch Cathedral, a wooden church at that time. Its other claims to fame are that it was in a concert hall about here that Handel gave his first rendering of the Messiah. It was also where Molly Malone wheeled her barrow "through streets broad and narrow singing cockles and mussels alive alive-oh."

The quayside was crowded with boat builders and repairers, sail-makers, coopers, rope-makers, warriors, some pilgrims and churchmen, and children everywhere lending a hand or getting in the way.

The city was surprisingly small - about forty acres at the most at the time of the Vikings. It was surrounded by a palisade of wooden stakes and dwarfed by the great ships on the waterfront below. The smells, sounds, smoke and filth of so congested a settlement can be imagined. There were many English silver pennies in circulation and merchants carried their own scales. The language at this date was a mix of Old Norse and Irish.

The great ships being unloaded here contained rare and beautiful artifacts from far and wide - silks from Byzantium and beyond, wines from France, ivory and furs from the Arctic, and lumps of amber from Baltic ports. Worsted and pottery vessels came from England, and ponies from Wales.

Cargoes being loaded for shipment abroad would feature fleeces, hides, marten pelts, cloth and some slaves. There was trade both ways in smaller items, such as jewellery, souvenirs and food products. Some iron weapons came from the continent of Europe but the Vikings were gradually turning away from violence to commerce and becoming integrated into the native population.

The artistic prowess of these primitive people, who lived in such squalor, is hard to credit. As a twentieth-century writer and poet, Stephen Gwynn, put it "Dublin is alive with her dead."

Reaching the summit

The wind ruffles my hair and the sun is warm on my stony seat. I have reached the summit of the mountain. My first mountain.

I climbed up here to find a cairn on the top and a note left within it for me by a favourite cousin; he who was the inspiration for all my youthful enthusiasm and who recognised that I needed the incentive, because I was a lazy girl, puppy-fat and idle.

The climb was strenuous enough, though in truth this long range is not much more than a line of hills. I have seen it every day from my window, explored its wooded foothills for foxes and red squirrels, birds nests and wild mushrooms.

Having pushed my way through bracken and loose stones, and clambered over boulders, I came to the final steep slope which opened out onto a grassy mound topped by the loosely built cairn on which I now sit.

I see the world anew.

The view is superb all around; the countryside bathed in sunshine with fleeing clouds and shadows. Every road and farmstead of my home-ground is laid out before me; the sheep and cattle, the smoke from the chimneys, and the BIRDS; larks singing above me, finches and crows, and the occasional kestrel hunting below. The sense of freedom, of space, is new to me, intoxicating. I can see now why people climb mountains; not just because they are there. This is the pay-off, this glory, this sense of "otherness", this quiet. No sound but the wind and the song of the lark.

I am very reluctant to go down again to the grimy world below.

A family picnic

When I was a child, sea-water was clean and transparent, full of creatures and bright sea-weed. Beaches were free from plastic and oil, and one could bring home shells and interesting pieces of washed-up timber. The rock pools held sea anemones and tiny crabs and shrimps. Our feet were always bare and almost web-toed! We seem in retrospect to have swum and picnicked all summer long. The days were always sunny and full of strawberries and ice-cream.

We didn't own a car in those days. Our pony and trap was driven by John who looked after the hamper and rugs, and saw that the picnic guests had everything they needed for their comfort. He had been my grandfather's batman in India. He and I were fellow-conspirators in all sorts of innocent pranks, though on this particular picnic it was my mother who thought up the mischief.

We had with us some aged relatives, not only a great-aunt and her family, but also a friend of my father's from Paris. He was a small, chubby and voluble man, with the exaggerated gestures of the typical Frenchman, and I took great delight in teasing him. He always responded so magnificently. Two things I did not like in the sea were jellyfish with their long stinging tentacles which left such painful, red weals, and the forests of bladderwrack which threatened to tangle me in their waving fronds. This beach proved to have both. Dead jellyfish lay about on the tide-line with the drying sea-weed and those maddening sand-hoppers.

The grown-ups wisely chose to lay out the picnic on a grassy slope higher up, while my cousin Olive and I disappeared to fish among the rock pools. After the meal, disgruntled at not having had a swim, we poked about among the dead jellyfish and I boldly threw one at George, our little French friend. He leapt up squealing and chased me with it, and much vivid French vernacular ensued. Eventually the hampers were packed up and we all climbed back into the pony trap, replete and sleepy from the fresh air and sunshine, and headed for home.

That evening, having washed, changed and chatted our way through pre-prandial drinks, we proceeded to the dining-room. Each place at table had been set with a separate covered plate to keep the contents warm. As each guest lifted their cover, neat fillets of plaice were revealed but when George lifted his, there lay a round, transparent jellyfish neatly decorated with parsley and lemon slices!

Our cottage in Carraroe

Our cottage in Carraroe, Co. Galway, was built in the 1940's, partly as a bolt-hole in case of invasion by the Nazis. The fall of France was a signal for retreat, and I think my father would have walked out into the Atlantic if it had come to that. He was not a fighter. He used to swim from the rocks in the early morning, looking white and skinny in the dawn light, creeping along among the sharp barnacles and slippery seaweed.

The cottage was built by local labour, including a skilled stonemason, who was a joy to watch as he fitted the blocks of granite together into an impressive fireplace. We had many painful collisions with it! The house also boasted a cellar and two Juliet balconies, the central living room being high to the rafters. The front porch looked out over Galway Bay to the Aran Islands.

We used to take trips to the Islands in the fishing trawlers with tarred sails, known as "hookers". This was quite an adventure in rough weather. If on the other hand one was becalmed it could take all day. We would sometimes fish for mackerel over the side, gutting them there and then, and cooking them below decks on an old primus stove. If one was not feeling sea-sick a mackerel never tasted so good, but on other occasions the smell was the last straw and when the boatman suggested we drank some of the bilge-water as a well-known cure, that finished us!

On one trip we had two donkeys on board which had been hoisted up by the sail ropes and lowered carefully on to the deck.

One very calm day we watched from the cottage the plight of some Ministers from the Dail Eireann and their wives in best city clothes and high-heeled shoes, becalmed for hours and becoming more and more desperate and dishevelled.

My father and his friend, Charles Lamb, the artist, would make forays into Galway in our little baby Austin, in search of rare bottles of Chateau d'Yquem, or more easily found pints of Guinness, and would return the worse for wear in the early hours.

In those days only one bus left Galway every day for Carraroe, and the passengers included marketing housewives and their baskets of live fowls, young students of the Irish language and English fishermen with their rods and boots. Other tourists, with their bulging rucksacks and the odd dog or two, were a pushing, shoving, scrambling mass, each one determined to get a seat at all costs. Queueing had not been invented. The young would initiate a sing-song. It became a lively journey of some thirty miles. It took a long time as the driver had to be refreshed with several pints on the way, but the arrival was worth it all, the air balmy and the view magnificent.

When my father first went to Carraroe, he travelled in the post bus and in 1951 my husband and I spent our honeymoon there. Now a modern hotel stands at the foot of the hill and I am loath to return in case I shatter the dream.

We did go back later on, not to Carraroe but to a friend's cottage at Cleggan.

The first thing that struck us, travelling west from the Shannon at Athlone was the widening of the sky; trees were sparse, buildings few and the rocky ground stretched to the horizon on all sides. There were lakes and turf-cuts in the bog, full of moving shadows and glittering water. I had forgotten how chilly the winds could be.

This time there were few thatched cottages. The new houses had electricity, telephones and Calor Gas. Deep-freeze cabinets had arrived and eggs and milk came in cartons. Cars and tractors had replaced donkeys on the bog. Fish farms were in evidence and rod licenses being introduced; not without a fight and some ill feeling. The Irish hospitality was warm as ever, but the locals were weary of change. Who can blame them for wanting to keep their dignity and their identity which so many people had lost already?

South Connemara, where Carraroe lies, had become more industrialised. We found our old

cottage rather gone to seed, a boat stuffed into the front porch; old cars and a mobile home, plus a modern bungalow, all in close proximity. It was all smaller than I remembered. Across the lane, a sculptor seemed to live, his yard full of strange, metal shapes resembling clockwork or flue brushes, strangely self-conscious and out-of-place in such a setting. Only the little harbour seemed unchanged. We came away; there was no-one there to detain us.

In North Connemara there were craft shops and one near us at Moyard, run by the Avoca Hand Weavers, was well worth a visit. We still appreciated the lovely soda-bread!

We found ourselves drawn to the ruined churches and tiny graveyards which abound there, containing the remains of so many fishermen drowned in the storms.

On one of our last days, we came upon a traffic accident. A schoolgirl lay in the road, her satchel propped against the stone wall. A bed had been made for her with a brightly-coloured blanket. Her mother knelt and stroked her hair while father stood guard and a small knot of people gathered round. When I asked if there was anything we could do, I was told "No"; and that monosyllable sounded very flat and final. This scene has etched itself on my memory and seems to symbolize all the qualities of patience and endurance which the years have bred into these people of the west.

It was a wet day when we set out for Galway and we did not linger, save for a bowl of delicious seafood chowder at O'Flaherty's bar beside the Great Southern Hotel, filled with the memorabilia of the old steam trains. Eyre Square now contains a fountain in which some schoolgirls were being dunked amidst wild screams and with many onlookers. As has been said many times, it is now a city for the young, and has an air about it. The shops include sports gear and video outlets; there is only one concession to Tweed O'Maille's which supplies jackets to the many thrusting young executives one sees about.

On our way through Athlone, we called into the church of St Peter and Paul to see the glorious stained glass windows by Harry Clark. They deserve a wider public.

Although Dublin was celebrating the Millenium that year, we had no time for any culture before our boat sailed.

Over the wall

Over the wall in Connemara there grazed a little grey donkey. It was a low wall and full of holes; put together without cement as all the walls are over there. Each little 'garden' as the locals euphemistically call them, has its own character. Some are by the sea and used to lay out the kelp to dry, which is then used as manure to nourish the tiny gardens of potatoes, grown on raised beds. These gardens have to be carefully picked over for stones and the sparse earth husbanded and enriched, mainly with the kelp, but also with the 'scree' from the top of the bog, where the turf is cut.

Our little donkey was used to carry the sods of turf from the bog in two panniers slung over his back. In the corner of his field there was a goodly stack of the stuff, ready to feed the winter fires for our cottage. In another corner was a wind-blown hawthorn tree, which was his only shelter. These trees are said to be fairy trees and to cut one down brings the family bad luck. No wonder, for they provide precious shade in this barren land.

When we first built our cottage there, during the Second World War, it was a 'phenomenon'. No-one had ever seen such luxury. We had central heating, run from a turf-burning range and a loo which flushed within the house, not at the bottom of the garden. Of course, there was a price to pay; no-one knew how these things functioned and plumbers had to be fetched from Galway, thirty miles away. We were always in trouble!

In those days there was very little money about and our gift of a small donkey-cart and harness was much prized by our neighbours. Now turf could be brought home much faster and the cart would meet us from the bus when we came to stay, with all our luggage for the summer holidays. The little donkey was kept very busy.

I went back to see these people recently and when I heard from them later they sent me photographs of our little donkey-cart, all painted up and still very much in use. Whether it is the same donkey or not I couldn't say. I believe they are long-lived beasts and I have never personally seen a dead donkey!

Escape

When we were small, Betty and I, we had the run of the farmyard. We would disappear into the hay barn and spend happy hours sliding and jumping through the soft bales, like a couple of kittens. Then we would splash about in the mill pond to cool off, or watch the cows being milked and beg for a cup of the warm, frothy milk from the pail.

We lost touch as school claimed us and afterwards Betty and her father moved away.

Her mother died young and Betty's father was a strict parent. He was rather overbearing and, in his care, Betty became a studious girl with plaits and glasses. I scarcely recognised her when she came to stay one summer holiday. We were in our late 'teens and whereas I was beginning to take an interest in clothes and boys, and enjoying the odd dance, Betty had "got religion". She would take me to church on Sundays and talk about the Scriptures and the Saints as though they were very much alive to her. Sometimes she looked very sad and would wander off on her own to pray and meditate.

We drifted apart again and the next time I heard of her she had become a Roman Catholic and joined a strict Order of nuns. Her father had died and her sister ran a small-holding in Scotland. One day, when my husband and I were out for a drive in the Hampshire countryside we decided to visit her in the Convent in Wimborne where she was now the Reverend Mother.

We were ushered into the waiting room and eventually into a small salon which was divided by a grille. Here Betty joined us, looking old and thin. Years had passed since our last meeting but slowly we re-established our friendship over a cup of tea. This was served on a tray which was put on a turntable and swivelled round through the grille, to allow us to take our cup without human contact. Betty told us a story of her trip to the local library; a treat afforded her in her senior position, once a month. She had on one occasion found a book written by my father and smuggled it out under her cloak, reading it avidly in the privacy of her cell. She found herself mentioned in it, and the fact that she had found favour there absolutely astonished her, and opened up a sluice-gate to her past.

She spoke about our carefree days of childhood as though they were yesterday. They were as fresh to her as the present moment. Then the bell rang and we were dismissed. She had to get to the Chapel for Evensong. I cried bitter tears for her on the way home. I felt that she had regretted her enclosed life and not found the peace she had expected in her escape from the things of this world.

Lament for Connemara

The power has come to the West, but the glory has gone. No more simple people in their shawls and their bare feet, with their big, sad eyes and a blessing on their lips. No more donkeys with panniers of turf, criss-crossing the bog. No sweet smell of the burning turf on the Atlantic wind. The fires have gone out.

The power has come, carried by lines of plastic cable swinging above stony, reed-filled fields, devoid of potatoes or pigs. Scattered here and there between - modern bungalows; green lawns and fountains; double-glazing and double garages. Not a soul to be seen; everyone's in Galway earning money to pay for the power. Yet they've lost their glory and their chickens.

Only tour buses roam the macadamed "boreen", like dinosaurs, looking for souvenirs, and filled with people who never knew the glory days. Oh, they were poor days, in the eyes of Mammon. Only God knows where the soul dwells.

This was the old Kingdom of Connaught. Its graveyards still dot the shore-line where the fishermen lived and died that men might eat. Their flimsy currachs tossed by the gales, the hookers tarred sails with their cargoes of seaweed and turf – all gone now to make way for fish-farms in Killary Harbour. River fishing today is hedged about with rules and licences.

The old ways are no more. The young don't miss them, I dare say.

The unexpected find

We were on holiday in County Waterford, staying with my sister-in-law and her family. Years ago it was, when we were all young. We went out strawberry-picking in the fields outside Dungarvan, our local town. The strawberries were luscious and numerous, and in no time at all, we had filled our baskets and our tummies.

We sat down on a grassy bank in the sun to eat our sandwiches and rest our backs. Rolling over and picking stalks of grass to play tunes, I noticed a strange-looking stone. I picked it up and put it in my pocket. Later in the day, we called in at a café in the town for a much-needed cup of tea before starting on the long cycle ride home. I took out my stone and invited everyone to guess what it was.

Yes, it was a lump of granite, smooth and rounded, but it had a strange pattern on it. Was it part of the eye of a huge fly? Surely not, because no fly was ever that big! Was it the seed-pod of an ancient flower? Well, maybe. No-one could decide. I put it back in my pocket.

I've still got that piece of granite amongst several small fossils. It sits on a conservatory window sill. Luckily, I asked my sister-in-law what she thought it was before she died. I think she gave the right answer.

This is what she said.

"Years ago, when Ireland was covered in forest trees, there were many wild bees swarming in those trees, and your stone is a piece of honeycomb. The tree it was in would have fallen into the bog and, over the millennia, been squashed down and heaved about until the bog was cut and the stony fields were laid bare. That is why this is such a wonderful place for strawberries, which love the acid soil."

And so my question was answered. I still treasure my little stone because it reminds me of those sun-filled days of yore in my beloved Waterford.

Carol Ann Duffy's poem "Bees" asserts that honey is art. It is an art that we neglect at our peril.

A memoir

Jonathan says my family tree is more like a spider's web and he is not far wrong. My late husband and I were related on one or two of the strands, which confuses the issue further. Mother came in from outside and probably saved our sanity.

She was born in Nenagh, Co. Tipperary. Her father was a railway engineer, but I only knew him as an old man with a beard, who dandled me on his knee and allowed me to play with his watch chain.

Granny Whitehead had a bun in her old age. She was fond of gardening. The apple orchard was under-planted with lily-of-the-valley and wild strawberries. She cooked substantial Sunday lunches for all the family in the back kitchen in William Street. Her gravy was out of this world – thick, dark and full of substance.

The front parlour was never used and had net curtains and an aspidistra. It was the original kitchen and had a huge old-fashioned range which was kept polished like a steam engine; all gleaming brass and blacklead. Granny belonged to an American-style religious sect called "Cooneyites", and on Sundays she went to their meetings. My cousin Olive and I preferred to go to Mass with the maid and we used to play at "Church" in the parlour, lighting candles and genuflecting – it was much more colourful.

Mother always said granny favoured the boys in the family and she got out whenever she could and went to stay with an uncle and aunt at a big farm house called "Lodge" in Puckane, a village nearby.

Uncle Bob (Atkinson) and Aunt Sis lived mostly in the big Tudor hall of a kitchen, with dogs, cats, chickens and so forth. The driveway was lined with cowslips and mother would love to bundle them into balls like the woollen ones we used to make.

Mother was happy there, and when she died I wanted to bury her in the little

graveyard at Cloughjordan, where her mother and Uncle Jack lie, but Dad said he wanted her in Dublin and so she lies there in a large cemetery where the Ussher family have a vault and other graves. My father lies sandwiched between her and his second wife whom he married in his seventies.

Mother had long, long hair as a child and boasted that she could sit on it. As a young woman she wore it in a knot. She was caught in a fire in her childhood and was always scared of fire thereafter. She rescued only her doll and two blue china mugs which I have still.

Olive was the daughter of her younger sister, Sally, who married Uncle George (Denroche). He was a cashier in the Provincial Bank. After their marriage they came back to the family home in William Street to help run the place until Uncle George was transferred to the Cork branch*. By this time Grandfather Whitehead had died and granny moved to Dublin to live with her unmarried son, Jack.

There were two other sons, Tom and Chris. Tom was also an engineer and worked in Sunderland, where he married his landlady. He invented jelly paint long before it became available, but was unable to promote it due to lack of funds.

Chris became a doctor and also made an unfortunate marriage. His wife was very young, pretty and vivacious. Chris was serious about his profession. They were divorced and Uncle Chris "took to drink" which finally killed him. He was buried in Wolverhampton where he had been working at the time.

Mother was originally in love with a doctor who was drowned in the Lusitania disaster. She always said proudly that he gave his life-jacket to another passenger. Shortly after this, she and a friend, Gladys Purdon, applied for jobs at the Ussher family estate

---

* *This house is now run as a B&B and Olive and her husband once booked in there unwittingly as the road name had changed. Great was their astonishment to find themselves so AT HOME while on holiday!*

in Cappagh, Co. Waterford. Gladys went as a secretary to my grandfather, and Mother as a companion-help to my grandmother. She ended up marrying their only son, Percy Arland, my father. My Grandmother Em (neé Jebb) says of her in a Journal – "In the Spring of 1918 God sent me my daughter, though I little knew what she would become to me more and more every year".

The 1920's brought the "Troubles" to Ireland, with the emerging Nationalists, the Black and Tans and the Workers' Strike. My grandfather was High Sheriff of the County. Grandmother was involved with the Irish Countrywomen's Association, the local Co-operative and the Dungarvan Show. Father claimed to be a pacifist; he was trying to learn Irish and to keep out of trouble with his father. The other "gentry" were mostly hunting, shooting and fishing types. Through all this my mother's common sense and humour steered a conciliatory course.

In April 1925, at the little church in Whitechurch she and my father were married. In January 1926, I was born. I had a younger brother but he was hydrocephalic and died when he was ten years old. This was a great sadness to my parents and it means that in our particular branch of the family the name of Ussher dies out.

My native river

My native river was the Blackwater in County Waterford. It was born in the foothills of the Knockmealdown Mountains. As a small stream it flowed through the wild rhododendrons and the sheep pastures north-west of Lismore. It flowed under the old lichen-covered stone bridges, becoming ever more forceful and producing deep pools and small waterfalls, clear, sparkling and full of life.

Then at Lismore Bridge it broadened out as it flowed under the castle ramparts and became a placid, brown, peaty flood following the road to Cappaquin, passing all the old country estates with their great houses. On to the sea it went, finishing up after taking a sharp right-hand bend in Youghal, where the film "Moby Dick" was made. Before my time, Youghal was the home town of Sir Walter Raleigh who brought us our potato, which was to play such a major role in our history and our diet.

I lived at Cappagh, which was slightly off the course of the river, though we had a couple of lakes from one of its tributaries in the grounds. On these lakes, I learned to fish for trout. An old retainer would take me out in the boat, tie flies for me with exotic names like Greenwell's Glory, Wickham's Fancy or Golden Oliver, and give me credit for more than my fair share of the catch. We would get stuck under bridges, shouted at by neighbours and eaten up by midges. We risked our lives dodging the bog holes in the surrounding countryside. We laughed a lot and got ourselves wet, cold and slimy with fish scales but then we had the fun of cooking and eating our own fish!

When I was older and married, we went to stay with my sister-in-law in Lismore and with our combined offspring, set out to camp among the sheep pastures in the valley. Here was a deep pool in which we could all swim, wash our cutlery and fetch fresh water for our kettle. One never-to-be-forgotten day, Tony announced "There are fish here!" and he set off home to fetch his flippers and a landing net. In he dived into the pool and came up with several beautiful sea trout in the net. One of the younger boys knocked them on the head with a stone; no qualms about that – they were country-bred. Of course it was poaching but one fish was earmarked for the police station. We had the other two for supper. I remember that meal as though it were yesterday, perhaps because it was a stolen treat, but more likely for its delicious flavour. However, the landlord had his revenge. Our camp-site was riddled with sheep tics which transferred themselves to us in all kinds of embarrassing places!

Nowadays the fishing on the Blackwater is world-renowned and enormously expensive. It is largely owned by the Duke of Devonshire at Lismore Castle. The other great houses have suffered various fates over the years, some demolished, others converted to hotels and a few still in private hands with their gardens open to the public. Our old home is still owned by the family who bought it from us over sixty years ago.

I look back on elaborate birthday parties and Christmas Balls as though from another planet, but the wild flowers, birds and days by the river were more to my taste and I am grateful to have grown up in those expansive times before the world changed for ever in the Second World War.

Dreaming of days gone by

In the heady days before the Second World War, the plan was for me to be educated at Bedford College in Regents Park. The Principal was at that time Geraldine Jebb, known to us as Gem, for she was a cousin. Whether I would have had the academic ability to be admitted – who knows? But the war intervened, I went to school in Northern Ireland and later trained to be a physiotherapist in Dublin, travelling up from Waterford but not having to cross the Irish Sea.

However I did visit Bedford College with my grandfather in those early years and it was my first time in England. I had forgotten entirely about it until recently when our daughter won a photographic competition to have a portrait done at a London studio. She asked me to come with her and we set off, armed with sandwiches for our lunch, as it would take time for the photographs to be developed. In fact, the whole performance took a very long time and I sat day-dreaming as I waited for her to emerge like a butterfly from a chrysalis.

We took our sandwiches up into Regents Park, to Queen Mary's Gardens. The roses were in bloom; the Regency Terraces had recently been refurbished and looked really opulent. There, covered in Virginia creeper, stood Bedford College. The years rolled away and I was a small child again.

Grandfather and I set out with some excitement in the pony and trap, laden with heavy suitcases in the early morning. On our way we met the donkey carts taking churns of milk to the dairy, which was opposite the local station. We bought our tickets; the steam train creaked to a halt and we were loaded in. The brass door handles clanked shut with a satisfying twist. We let the window down on its leather strap and said our goodbyes. We were off on the great adventure. My feet barely reached the floor of the carriage and I remember the seats being horribly prickly under my bare knees. Cases were lifted onto the luggage rack and I surveyed the pictures of ancient Irish castles and sandy beaches which decorated the walls.

Several hours later we pulled in to Kingsbridge Station beside that famous brewery alongside the River Liffey. Here we transferred to a cab and with the assistance of a well-tipped porter and another trotting horse eventually came to the mail-boat pier at Dun Laoghaire, or Kingstown as it then was.

I was always horribly sea-sick as a child, usually before the boat had left the harbour, so I presume I started as I meant to go on. Mercifully, I don't remember. My only recollections of the journey to London are of the Irish mail train clanging its way through that long tunnel outside Birmingham; (later on, we owned that lovely old record by Reginald Gardiner, and he describes it exactly) and then the train coming in to London through all those suburbs and tiny back gardens which seemed to go on for ever. I began to wonder what I had let myself in for! By the time we had reached Gem's flat in one of those Regency terraced houses I mentioned earlier, I was pretty tired.

Memories are jumbled of those few days; elaborate meals with some ceremony, huge bath-tubs with great brass taps and old-fashioned shower systems, freezing linen sheets on beds so high I had to climb in. Tours around the college classrooms were followed by walks in those rose gardens. Cousin Gem was a lovely person with twinkling eyes and I was forced out of my shell in no time. Even better, she had a house-keeper called Edith, who saw that I got all the tit-bits the extra meringue or another chocolate biscuit, or whatever. She ran my bath for me, tucked me up at night and generally spoiled me rotten!

After Gem died, Edith went to work for her sister and we met again forty odd years ago when we finally came to live in England. Now she spoiled our daughter, taking her to see "The Sound of Music" instead of a tour of the Oxford Colleges as my cousin had suggested. The strange thing was that as we sat eating our sandwiches in Queen Mary's Gardens, Edith lay dying.

I didn't know at the time and I hadn't visited Regents Park since those long-ago days of childhood. Life is full of those strange coincidences and they fascinate me.

At Edith's funeral, the organ played the theme tunes from "The Sound of Music" and daughter and I had a little weep as our memories collided once again.

Favourite trees

I was born in a house called The Giant's Rock in County Waterford, Southern Ireland. It stood on a hill-top above a spinney of Scots Pine. In these trees frolicked a whole fir-cone team of red squirrels; lovely little creatures now so seldom seen. Early on, I read Beatrix Potter's story of Squirrel Nutkin who lost his tail to Old Brown, the owl across the lake. As there were owls in this wood, I could visualize Nutkin's fate only too clearly.

When I grew a little older, I was fascinated by the story of a squirrel who planted a cone which grew into a great jackpine. It was written by "Grey Owl", that supposedly North-American Indian who has since been found to be of Kentish origin, but whose wild-life tales were nonetheless beautifully told. This story, played out beneath the branches of the jackpine, was about the adventures of an Indian Brave and a grizzly bear. Finally the tree is felled to make way for a new highway across the plain; however not before another squirrel has planted a cone by the wayside. Was this an early intimation of immortality for me? Nowadays it perhaps has a modern message for Swampy; the power of nature to compensate for our indiscretions.

Elsewhere on that estate, there was another favourite tree connected with my early years, a weeping elm which drooped over a terrace outside the house. One hot summer, having discovered its privacy and shade, I decided that my toys should share it with me. Out came Tommy and Teddy, Lucy and "The Hare", a strange, knitted creature which my father would stick out of reach in a jug on the dresser. I did not appreciate his warped sense of humour. Out also came stools and tea sets, a piece of lino and even a potty. Great was my embarrassment when in the autumn the leaves fell off!

During school-days, there were many favourite trees for climbing and for building tree houses. The spreading branches of oaks and beeches were often invaded, playing out scenes from "The Swiss Family Robinson" or "Treasure Island". Favourite vantage points emerged and cosy crannies to curl up in. Special hand-holds and foot-holds became shiny with much use. Picnic spots beneath candelabra of chestnut spikes were cleared of nettles and sharp stones. I tested the theory that leaning against the bole of a mighty tree and telling it one's troubles was a soothing thing to do.

After marriage came a honeymoon in Connemara among rowan trees, with their spectacular red berries, which looked wonderful in a large brass bowl on the granite fireplace. There were also magic, fairy hawthorn circles where we wished for eternal happiness and good fortune. It was outside our first cottage and home for over twenty years near Belfast that I met my first Wellingtonia. Its lofty bulk towered above our garden. It was a homing device for all the family. On Coronation Day, my intrepid husband climbed to the top and attached a Union Jack to flutter in the breeze.

On moving to England, I discovered that the Cedar of Lebanon was one of the most majestic trees in existence. I was lucky enough to see one every day as I drove to work. Geese wandered at its feet and swallows flew about its head. In the evenings on my way home, it was often silhouetted against the sunset, giving it even more shape and form. As I looked out from my kitchen sink, there was a golden acacia, planted by neighbours on their fiftieth wedding anniversary. Behind this, a row of silver birches reflected the sunlight from their mottled bark, their branches feathering the sky. Another rare treasure that I could see from the window was a black poplar.

Very tall and gaunt in winter, its leaves in summer made a wonderful rustling sound, just like running water. Black poplar was once used in the construction of farm wagons and for making wooden bowls. Now there are only fifteen hundred trees at most surviving here. The Tree Council and Forestry Commission are taking steps to preserve them, so I was fortunate to have one so close.

A more sombre friend in Selborne was an ancient church-yard yew. Reputed to be about fourteen hundred years old according to its girth and rings, it finally keeled over during the great storm of January 1990. Although cleverly re-instated by experts it did not survive. All is not lost however. A new sapling from its seed is flourishing nearby assuring its immortality just like that of the jackpine. Many beautiful artifacts have been made from its broken timbers. Under its roots a quantity of bones were unearthed, including seven complete skeletons which have been re-interred in fresh graves.

Now that I have moved into town, I like sometimes to sit under the apple tree in the market square while perusing a book from the library or demolishing a hot dog from one of the market stalls.

It would be pleasant if I could be finally laid to rest under the shade of a tree and near where people linger; within the orbit of an acorn, a fir cone or a crab-apple!

Running free

When Dervla Murphy was ten years old her father gave her two presents – a bicycle and an atlas. At the time she was running free over the hills, pushing through the heather and the bracken, collecting mushrooms and wild flowers and bathing in the river which ran through the village. The bicycle, however, brought more ambitions and soon she was poring over the atlas, planning journeys to exotic places.

She began with Europe. Her mother had told her stories of Isabella of Castile and Teresa of Avila. Her grandfather was a Cervantes addict and he had read to her from the stories of Don Quixote. And so in 1956 she headed for Spain, where she stayed in cheap "pasadas" and found a soothing affinity with the Spaniards. On the open plains she found a sense of remoteness and solitude which was very much to her taste.

She didn't stop there. Her big ambition was to ride from Dunkirk to New Delhi and on to the foothills of the Himalayas. She was able eventually to make this trip and the epic story of her journey is told in her books "Full Tilt" and "Tibetan Foothold". It wasn't until she was almost thirty that she was free to make this trip. Her mother had become very ill when Dervla was in her late teens, and she had nursed her for sixteen years. During this period, her father died and Dervla herself had a complete breakdown. The freedom, when it came, though, left no bitterness. Family love had endured it all and walking around her newly acquired cottage Dervla comments that "Unexpectedly I found myself revelling in the novel sensation of ownership". She converted her mother's bedroom into a study, replacing the bed with her desk, and it was here that she wrote her travel books. They are many and inspirational. Her father had been the County Librarian and the house was always full of books.

Dervla still lives in Lismore, Co. Waterford and has become as much a part of the fabric of the town as the Cathedral or the Castle. This is in itself a small miracle but to find out the "whys and wherefores" you will have to read her book "Wheels within Wheels", an autobiography of her early years.

What lies down that path?

The path in question was always called "the track" in our family. It led down to a lake, Lough Dan, in Co. Wicklow, just south of Dublin.

Family associations go back and back. The latest discovery was that an ancestor of mine danced across the stepping-stones to the strains of a fiddle in 1832! In those days, there was a community of "cabins" around the lake and on Sundays the young of the village, in their "Sunday blue" would congregate by the river and dance. My ancestor was on a walking holiday, staying with relatives nearby, and wrote a journal of his trip which I recently discovered. Up to that discovery, all the associations had been on my husband's side. He first came to Lough Dan in 1928. The lake and the mountainside around it was, and still is, owned by the Archer family, Ford motor dealers in Dublin.

My husband's family had "carte blanche" to camp out there whenever they wanted. I believe when Gerry and his brother Richard first camped there they left the place so tidy they were forever welcomed back. They made themselves agreeable by helping to chop logs and by catching little brown trout for the family breakfasts.

Over the years, there were many bonfire picnics, boating excursions and swimming in the brown, boggy lake waters. The lake has a lovely beach and a big log to sit on by the lakeside bungalow. Other family "shacks" are dotted about the sides of the track. Organically grown as the family increased, they seem to mushroom out of the hill. We used to borrow one called "The Haven". It was a log cabin with a corrugated iron roof and a balcony at either end – rather like a wild-west

train. Inside were army surplus bedsteads with stripy cotton blankets and precarious overhead shelves full of paper-backs and magazines. In the other room was a black, wood-burning range, a scrubbed table, assorted chairs and a few orange-boxes with cooking pots, plates and cutlery. All "mod cons" were in the great out-doors, and water had to be fetched from a "spout" down the track a bit. One had to brave the horse-flies and midges on the way and it was not a popular chore. The water was clear and cold off the mountain and never dried up. We used to refresh ourselves by washing our hair under it before filling the cans.

Our younger daughter and her husband started their honeymoon in one of the Archer family's cabins, and in the year 2000 my husband's ashes were scattered at the stepping-stones. Afterwards, both daughters and I had a nostalgic lunch-party with the family, looking at all the old visitors' books and re-living many happy times. It was a golden day, with gorse blooming everywhere and birds singing.

The future of the family ownership there is precarious but is helped financially by film companies using the place quite often. Our friend Hilary was very amusing, telling us of her encounter with a robot pig by the lake-shore, during the making of "Animal Farm".

I look forward, as ever, to my next drive down the track and hope it may be soon.

Murder in the glen

Have you ever been involved in a murder case? Believe me, it is both frightening and fascinating, like an Agatha Christie novel in the making. Always provided, of course, that you know you are innocent and have faith in good old-fashioned British justice.

Murder was not an every-day occurrence in 1952, even in Northern Ireland, but it was in that year on a foggy November night that we were woken at 2 a.m. by frantic knocking on our cottage door. We had been married a year and a half and our first-born was nine months old. We lived in a tied cottage which we subsequently bought. The big house was at the bottom of a steep wooded glen and we lived at the top, looking after the walled garden of the estate and running it as a market garden. The big house was owned by a High Court Judge. He had a wife, two sons and a daughter. It was the younger son, Desmond, who was hammering on our door in the middle of the night.

When my husband, Gerry, came back to bed, he told me that Desmond wanted to borrow a torch; his sister Patricia had not turned up at home from college and that as a last resort he wanted to search the glen. For some reason, Gerry did not offer to go along. He had had a hard day ploughing up some-one else's garden with a large rotovator, a circumstance we were subsequently grateful for. Yes, you've guessed, because Desmond found his sister's body amongst the trees at the side of the drive-way. Her beret and books were laid quite tidily on the path but she had been stabbed more than twenty times.

Later, the Judge (her father) and the family solicitor, who was an old and valued friend, put the body in the family car and took it to the doctor's surgery. The story was that when Desmond lifted her, she had sighed and they had thought she was still alive. It was a strange thing for professionals of the law to do; yet who knows how one would react in such a situation?

Gerry had often seen Patricia home when she would join us for tea, having taken the bus further on through the village, perhaps to do some shopping or simply to chat and see our baby. She was a gregarious seventeen-year-old. We questioned why Desmond had not contacted us earlier.

Next day we decided to stay close to the house; a madman may have been lurking in our midst, and anyway we expected that the police would want to interview us. We phoned my mother, who came up from Dublin for reassurance and stayed a few days with us. Sure enough, in the afternoon a local policeman came round. Later, Chief Inspector Capstick of the Yard entered the case.

"What kind of knife do you use in the garden?" was their first question. Eventually, exasperated, Gerry mentioned his relationship to the Northern Ireland Chief of Police, Dick Pim. A likely story, they thought, and pressed him further.

Weeks later they made an arrest; a young man from the local army unit, who made a confession in police custody, but he had not been supported by his family or his Commanding Officer. The term "unsafe" had not then been conjured up, but this conviction was clearly that. Eight years later, the young man was quietly released.

For us though, this was only the beginning. The Sunday papers got hold of the story and we were pursued by reporters. They were likeable young men and we allowed them to take photographs and gave them coffee. They would chat to us about our past, separately, and then cross-check our stories. They were completely unscrupulous and went so far as to phone up Gerry's parents, telling them that Gerry was going to broadcast a programme on gardening, and asking if they could provide some background information. It did not take us long to work out who the crazy callers had been, and we henceforth kept our own counsel.

Next to appear was an elderly lady with a mission. She worked for a prisoners' aid society or some such worthy body. She was very long-winded and became rather a bore. We felt bound to listen, as we thought justice had quite possibly not been done, and that it could so easily have been Gerry who had been picked on, but for his cast-iron alibi.

Months later, the young man's family hired a private detective to pursue the cause of establishing his innocence, and we had all the questions over again. This man unearthed blood stains in Patricia's bedroom. By now, Glen House was occupied by an even more colourful family and when the 'tec visited us they exhorted us not to let him get away. "Let down his tyres" they advised. I forget now why. I'm not sure I ever knew. Eventually, the Sunday Times Supplement published an article on the case, in which we were mentioned, but that was the end of our moment of notoriety.

The speculation continues to this day. Patricia's brother, Desmond, became a priest and went off to Rome, subsequently ending up in Africa. He had always been a searcher, at one time belonging to a Moral Rearmament Group. He and Patricia were very close. Had she perhaps rumbled the fact that he was also a homosexual and threatened to tell their father?

We shall never know.

Ripples around Louis Macniece

At the end of their lives, my friends John and Leila Rawlings moved to a house in Melksham, Wiltshire, there they had on their wall a picture of Louis Macniece with his borzoi dog, Betsy. It was an early etching by Jack Yeats of Connemara in the glory days and I loved it.

Let me explain. The Macnieces originally came from Connemara and, as a teenager, it was the place I loved above all other. Gerry and I spent our honeymoon there. The Macnieces moved to Northern Ireland and when, later on, our two daughters went to prep school in Belfast, it was John Rawlings who was their headmaster. He and Gerry also ran the local Air Training Cadets Unit. Leila Rawlings was Louis Macniece's aunt. She was a warm-hearted woman, a real headmaster's wife, without whom no school could function.

We four were good friends. John studied the horses and loved to go to the point-to-point meetings, but it was usually Gerry and I who bought the supper, our horses having been chosen solely on their looks!

Louis Macniece's father was a bishop, but they were not close – Louis always felt he had let the side down but after his father's death he regretted this bitterly. Yet strangely the same state of things existed between Louis and his son, Dan, who followed his mother to America after their divorce.

It was Louis' father who officiated at my grandfather's second marriage. This wedding took place on the day that I should have started at a new school. Instead I went to the ceremony with my parents. When I turned up at school the next day and explained that I had been to my grandfather's wedding, everyone thought I was being fresh and thus got a very false impression of my character – so important among schoolgirls! I never thought to explain that it was his second marriage. Moreover, my present partner, Jonathan and I, got together as well, at much the same age! Anyhow, when my mother and father came out from the church, everyone thought they were the bride and groom, and threw their confetti too early, thereby creating some very awkward moments!

Thus it was that I was introduced to the Macniece family circle without ever really getting to know the poet, except through reading his work which I now enjoy the more because of these associations. Louis was a great drifter, always wanting to stay on or move on, unlike his disciplined writing. He would sing:-

"Goodbye Lily and goodbye Kate.
If I'm not home early then I'll be late.
I'll give you a kiss and go my way
And I'll see you again on Judgement Day."

The meeting place

When I first went to work at Forest Mere in 1976, it was a private health farm owned by Ken Wood of Mixer fame. Its general manager, Tim Grey, was a friend of my boss, Joan Schonfeldt. They hailed from South Africa. It became a meeting place for the great and the good, the royals, film stars, theatre people and wealthy divorcees. Marriages were made there, and broken. Many survivors of the Jewish Holocaust gathered there, laughing at themselves for paying good money to be starved.

As physiotherapists, we were privy to their inner thoughts and hopes, their weird life-styles and their private fears. This was because they knew that their secrets were safe with us. We would not have dreamed of selling their stories to the newspapers. Helicopters landed on the lawn. I was once invited to Paris in one for lunch!

The work as such was not that interesting; nothing like a hospital department. It was more a matter just of back-aches, head-aches, drink-related illnesses, excesses of one kind and another, or the need for a sympathetic ear or a relaxing massage. I spent eight years there and my husband joined me, working part-time in the gardens. We would have lunch together in the canteen. The house-keeper, Barbara Hopkins, came from Galway and gave us large salads to take home for our supper.

I met so many people that now I rarely see an old film, or hear about a politician or visit a stately home that does not connect in my mind with some incident or conversation from my past. It makes life interesting. Of course there were embarrassing moments too. There were several theatrical people who liked to walk about in various stages of nakedness, and those who brought their dogs with them, or their drink problems. I believe there was even a murder but that was before my time.

During that time everything changed so much and eventually the place was sold to the Savoy Group. Since then it has had a fire, a rebuild and another take-over. It is now owned by Champney's, a chain of health resorts. It has a more sporty clientele and greater emphasis on exercise and youth. Yet no doubt it is still a meeting place of some renown.

I could go on, but I'm really only covering up the fact that, despite having touched the lives of so many of the world's celebrities, I am the only one to have never done anything very memorable in mine!

These memories though have brightened my hours in front of the television and given life a wider dimension.

Family album

There is nothing quite so nostalgic as a photograph album. Especially one which holds pictures of one's offspring. The first shots of a new-born baby lying on a rug, or nestling in proud Mother's arms. Then the christening in a long, lacy gown, with adoring relatives all dressed up and paying homage. After that there is an intimate peep at Emily, naked on the lawn, looking over her shoulder and saying "ooh!" in a most knowing way. That's very non-PC these days.

There is a pink fairy Jacqueline going to a party, with her ballet shoes in a bag; oh, and the two of them in fancy dress; one a doll, the other a gollywog with a blackened face, made with a burnt cork and shoe polish. The caption "No colour-bar in toyland"; they won a prize for that one.

Then came schooldays and shot of two little girls holding hands, satchels over their shoulders, bright new blazers. Butter wouldn't melt. Sunday school in neat hats and "Startrite" shoes, and the Saturday gang holding a garage sale for charity. I can't remember their names any more, but one or two have stayed the course. Sports Day sees them all in blue bloomers. The red team and the green; a three-legged race and the egg and spoon. Such concentration on their faces as one rarely sees now.

Emily in her nightie getting eleven-plus results from the postman. I remember him saying "You're OK, you've got the fat envelope."

Jacqueline in her ball dress after graduation – the one her Canadian uncle bought her in Liberty's of London.

There are some pages of holiday snaps. Catching crabs in the rock-pools, and picnicking by the lake at Lough Dan. A visit to the zoo with my parents – Jacqueline on a pony ride. Emily cooking buns and offering them round. Her dad letting off fireworks at Hallow E'en, and climbing the big tree in front of our cottage, to place a flag on the top for the Coronation. Now he has gone to claim his wings, and Emily and Jackie are past the half-way mark I'm starting a new chapter, but also collecting pictures of my grand-child, Juliet, and my great-grand "steppies".

Granny is allowed her "Boasting Books".

Oakshott

Oakshott Hanger is a bowl of beech trees clinging to the hillside near Petersfield. Halfway up is the wonderful arts-and-crafts style cottage built by Dr Roberts. He was the local, well-known philanthropist who endowed the Festival Hall. At Oakshott he set up a retreat for TB sufferers from London's East End where he had spent his working life. He built huts among the trees where his patients could live a quiet, out-door life. He himself lived in the cottage with his house-keeper and his secretary.

After Dr Roberts' death, the place was auctioned by Jacobs & Hunt and it was bought by friends of ours, Roger and Kathleen Field. Roger was a direct descendant of Oliver Cromwell whose portrait hung in the dining room at Oakshott. Kathleen owned an antique shop where Tesco Direct now stands. She had been a family friend since her college days, having been to Trinity in Dublin with my father.

To return to the subject of the auction, the story goes that Roger and Kathleen became separated and afterwards Roger said "That was a lovely house. We should have bought it." Kathleen replied "But we did!" So it was that we came to stay there with them on holiday from Northern Ireland. Much later, during that wonderful summer of 1976, we lived there with Kathleen for six months. It was an education, an idyll and an endurance test.

"Outy, outy, outy?" she would cry every evening and the seven Pekinese would scurry to the terrace door for the evening ramble. They were a feisty bunch of dogs and we grew to love them. The two cats, Demon and Cosset, sleek, black hunter and whining white ball of fluff, had a never-ending supply of mice amongst the undergrowth on the hill-side and loved to bring them indoors to play with and leave half-dead under the cushions.

Our bedroom sloped into the rafters and housed a Blue Period Picasso, amongst other delights. Kathleen's room across the landing had a balcony overlooking the kidney-shaped swimming pool with a view across the trees to Butser Hill. On a clear day, one glimpsed the sea beyond. Here we would gather for breakfast and the morning rituals of post and papers, shopping-lists and phoning friends. The cats curled up on Kathleen's bed. The dogs slept at the back of the house and Kathleen erected a screen across the landing to keep them there. Unfortunately, our bathroom was at the other side of this and I invariably forgot, and clattered into the blessed thing, waking everybody up!

The back corridor was lined with large, heavy paintings of inestimable value and so it was a relief to reach the small room at the end. This looked directly onto the hillside. In the early morning one could lean on the heater under the window to watch the squirrels leaping from tree to tree and listen to owls hooting. An occasional fox would slink by or a pheasant would call out. The wine cellar was let into the hillside below and some wonderful vintages were produced to accompany the gourmet parties that Kathleen often gave.

She professed to be a "Cordon Bleu" cook. However, one evening she produced pink mashed potatoes for our small daughter's supper, which she did not appreciate. Later, in the cupboard, I came across puppy medicines which she had used to colour them!

In summer, meals were taken on the terrace under a canopy of vine leaves looking out to a Chinese statue under a drooping maple tree, sipping a Pimm's or an after-dinner glass of port. It was a truly idyllic way of life.

All this came at a price though, as Kathleen went into hospital at the old Q.A. leaving us to cope with it all, the shopping, dog grooming and endless phone calls and taking her post every day to the hospital, We looked after a very odd Irish gardener and picked buckets of walnuts from two beautiful trees which later came down in the 1980's hurricane. There were also mulberries and pears which grew away out of reach. My husband risked his life on the rickety ladder on the hillside to retrieve them. Wild raspberries and strawberries grew everywhere among the grass.

After Kathleen was discharged from QA, we had nurses to please as well for a while and then our two daughters came on holiday. In the end, we decided it was time to call a halt and Kathleen helped us buy a flat in Liss.

We moved just in time for Christmas and rediscovered the joys of being our own sovereign selves again on our own more modest budget. We all remained friends.

The reunion

They were married in the 30's. A stylish couple – the young doctor dedicated and hard-working; his wife chic and pretty, almost a "flapper".

He built up a thriving practice amongst the affluent population of the seaside suburbs where they lived, and in the course of time they had three children, two girls and a boy. Their house was solid and formal, and had a slight whiff of disinfectant about it from the doctor's consulting room-cum-study. His desk and book shelves, potted plant and net curtains made it seem brooding. The dining room also was solemn and rather unused, with its glassware and decanters of sherry and whisky and its hunting prints. The sitting room was ultra-comfortable with deep armchairs and coffee tables of glossy magazines, but it was the adjoining conservatory that was the hub of the house and led into the terraced garden with steps and 'seaside' formal planting, leading to the beach.

Once the children had grown and gone off to school, the marriage deteriorated and they were divorced. Divorce in those days in Catholic Ireland was rare and uncompromising. No weekly access for fathers, with visits to the zoo or the cinema. It was a total break and, in this case, complete heartbreak. The doctor's practice suffered and he sold up his house, moved to England and took a hospital post. Gradually, his depression led him into alcoholism and he died alone in Wolverhampton in the 1950's.

Shortly after my husband died in the last months of the 20th century, I received a letter from one Yvonne Moore, who said she thought we might be first cousins. She had seen Gerry's death reported in the Irish Times and recognised my name. She would very much like to get in touch. The doctor of the tale was my uncle, and she was his eldest daughter, a great favourite of my mother's when we were all young. It was a sadness that Mother was now no longer alive to share in this reunion. My two daughters and I visited her and her family in Dublin and they entertained us in a big kitchen, with an Aga cooker and a large, scrubbed table with enough room for a family get-together. Her garden was a delight and flowers were everywhere; a happy, jolly household.

She helped me over my grief at Gerry's death with long, newsy letters, photographs of the various young families – all my new-found cousins – and Dublin medical gossip. It seems she was a medical secretary there when I was training to be a physiotherapist and we must have walked the same hospital corridors and met the same people without ever meeting each other. Her children's godmother was one of my college tutors!

I'm hoping that when Jonathan I go on holiday to Ireland we may meet up again for a meal and keep the reunion going.

A Currabinny holiday

No past or future here,
Just present Paradise.
Ten days out of time
Observing lazy rituals
Preserved religiously.

Early morning tea
In my sunny, seaward bedroom.
Boats ride at anchor, while
A heron makes his daily flight
The pier is empty of all life.
No sound disturbs the stillness.

Breakfast taken on the lawn, and
As we watch, the harbour comes to life.
Fishing boats get under way.
Seagulls whirl and dip.
Customs and the ferry pilot greet the day.

A walk, or gentle shopping trip,
Buying post-cards, fruit and bread.
Coffee to revive us for the chores
Of getting lunch; taking out the chairs.
Neighbours look in for a chat.
We watch the sails unfurl.

There goes a Westerly.
Oh look, the Optimists
Being towed in line.
Wave to Roy and Arthur in the Maestro.
(They'll never make it back in time for tea.)

Siesta with a book
Followed by a drive to Roche's Point.
Get ready for the party later on.
Neighbours all invited.

Wild flowers scent the room.
Arthur, one of "Nature's Gentlemen"
Reminisces on the old Lismore.
Ronnie's eightieth birthday toasted.

The evening light's so beautiful.
Just one more drink.
Let's take it on the pier.
The children have gone home now, and
All the many craft are coming in.

Tomorrow's for nostalgia –
Richard's ninetieth lunch-date in Lismore:
My old home and the Strand at Ardmore.
We're tired with all this effort, but content.

To Ballycotton for a final picnic on the rocks.
Ballymaloe House and tea with Myrtle Allen.
Presents from the tempting shop for those at home.
Currabinny has worked magic once again,
Rivalling Lough Dan in my affections.

Soon every-day life must resume its pace –
Airports, re-unions, England's cut-and-thrust.
So much awaits, but we are stronger,
Re-directed, calm, at peace.

A closure and a bonding all in one.

Little Stodham House

The original owners of Little Stodham House were the Money family. They owned many of the local fields and grew mint for the mint julep industry, which was big in Liss at that time. (Hence Mint Road, Mint Cottage, Mint Laundry). The original house was on the old Drovers route from the Harrow Inn to Rake, and was built of wattle and daub. It was later rebuilt in the Georgian style. Later still, a Victorian porch and rear section were added, with stables and servants quarters to the side.

Stodham Park Estate was owned by the Dorman-Smith family. Colonel Reginald Dorman-Smith held a high-ranking diplomatic post in the Far East. The coming of the railway bisected the estate in 1857.

During the war years Stodham Park House was used by the SOE (Special Operations Executive) as a centre for training operatives to carry out secret espionage missions in Europe. It was later bought by the Burtons (of Fifty Shilling Tailor fame) and has since been divided into smaller units.

Little Stodham estate included both the walled-in kitchen garden where the Hillyer Garden Centre is now located, and Stone Cottage which incorporated the boiler-house. The sunken garden, with its elaborate drainage system and sluice gates to the stream, was a show piece. There were many exotic plants such as a monkey puzzle tree, and numerous rhododendrons and azaleas, plus alpine plants brought from abroad. Tall Wellingtonias stood guard by the gates, as they do today.

Little Stodham was later used as a dormitory for pupils from Petersfield School. The grammar school was within the town and was short of space.

In more recent years the house was owned by, among others, an aunt of a certain Mrs Goor, and thereby hangs a strange tale of coincidence. Three years ago, a friend and I were travelling to Ireland on the Swansea-Cork ferry. We happened to share a table in the restaurant with another couple and we got into conversation. They were from Alton and going across to Kerry which they did four or five times a year as Mr Goor was a Kerry man. When I mentioned Little Stodham Mrs Goor's eyes lit up in recognition. She said the house had been owned by her aunt and she had visited many times during her childhood. We exchanged addresses but have never followed up.

About fifty years ago, Little Stodham was divided into six flats by an uncle of Peter Cooper's. Peter and his wife Wendy bought Number One and Wendy, now widowed, still owns it though she no longer lives there. We bought flat 5 and were very happy there. I lived there alone for several years after Gerry's death.

Despite the fact that Little Stodham House now sits in an enclave bounded by an iron perimeter to the north by the railway and to the south by the mighty A3 trunk road, it remains to this day reminiscent of its past and remarkably like a small country house with a rich abundance of wild life in its gardens.

Is there a God?

Is there a God
Or only this deep cavern at my feet?
My dear one's gone
To be a part of nature, that he loved.
The man I knew, who shared my life, withdrew.
I had to shout bald messages into thin air.
The tender, patient gardener, fun-loving 'Daddo',
Easy-going, happy half of me, became
Unrecognisable, then, no more.

I must go back,
Re-visit places that we found together.
Pilgrimage shall be my starting point
To live alone. Yet, not alone.
Each day, supported by my family and friends
He leads me on,
Treading softly thro' my dreams,
With Yeats, or Beethoven, or the Harvest moon,
His world a harmony
Within the music of the spheres.

On impulse

Samuel Beckett said: "We spend our life trying to bring together in the same instant a ray of sunshine and a free bench."

I was walking through the park when, ***on impulse***, I sat down on a free bench. The sun was hidden behind a cloud but I reckoned it might soon emerge. People were walking their dogs (all on leads), patiently waiting for them to relieve themselves, then scooping up the mess and putting it in a litter bin – or not.

Fishermen were angling in the pond, throwing back their catch for another day's sport. Joggers were panting past, their bellies wobbling and bosoms heaving but I just sat, waiting for the sun to emerge from the cloud.

Then you came along and sat beside me and smiled and ***on impulse*** you said what a joy it was to be able to share a park bench with such a serene person, and the sun shone in my heart again.

The cloud had lifted.

A significant building

I wonder if you have ever been to the Watts Chapel and Gallery at Compton, along with the house Limmerslease where J F Watts and Mary Watts lived and worked in the Great Studio. It is an inspiring place and has come to be a little bit entangled in my family history and my soul.

It was here that Jonathan and I first realized that we wanted to stay together. We met for tea at the café one day, Jonathan coming from Fleet and me from Liss. Having toured the Gallery and Chapel, we took a walk up the sandy lane at the back. We didn't want to part and go our separate ways.

I had been here years earlier with my father; again with cousins and other family members but this was only the beginning of my association with the place. My cousins did a bit of research and sent me the following dedication to my great grandmother:-

> *A Key to the Symbols on the Walls of the Chapel at Compton by Mrs G F Watts*
>
> *To Eglantyne Jebb who by the gift of sympathy first called about her a little gathering of workers from her village to practise the beautiful art of wood carving, and from which beginning sprang the union of many workers forming the Association of the Home Arts and Industries; these few pages, endeavouring to explain the spirit in the work done by us at Compton for our Chapel, are dedicated with love and gratitude.*

By this time I was packing up the flat at Liss and there was a screen in the hallway which none of the family could accommodate. I hadn't been able to get it upstairs as it was made of solid oak and had embossed leather panels executed by my great grandmother, Mary Watts' friend. I didn't want to sell it for the auction valuation of £600 so I contacted the Curator at Watts Gallery, an elderly man who was about to retire. At that time the Gallery was really dilapidated and threatened with closure. To cut a long story short, we finally arrived there with the screen in the back of a four-by-four, on the same day as his removal van. He was delighted with the screen and it was secreted in a little back office which was the only dry room in the place. There it remained for several years while the Gallery was putting in its bid for "Restoration" money. It only came second but the good news was that they could now qualify for a Lottery Fund grant the following year. After work had eventually started, the restorers went bust and work was restarted with a new firm.

The new Curator and the Director are live wires and have gathered around them an unbelievable team of volunteers. The Donor Board gets longer by the week and now my cousin, Lionel Jebb, has his name on it.

They have been able to use the Studio at Limmerslease for storage and hope to be in a position to buy back the entire house for the Trust. It is a race against time. My screen has now found its way there and we have been to see it. It has not yet been refurbished but we have drafted a note of explanation to be displayed with it, as follows:-

> *This decorative screen, circa 1890s, was crafted by Eglantyne Louisa Jebb, the Founder of the Home Arts and Industries Association. A keen follower of arts and crafts movements, the Association grew from her desire to revive traditional rural crafts and to relieve rural poverty. Mrs Jebb was an influential friend to Mary Watts and Mary dedicated her book "Word in the Pattern" to her friend in 1904.*

So you can see why for me this is a significant place. Indeed it is an important link in the development of art and culture in this country.

A red letter day

One day in the early 1990's I answered an advertisement from the Farnham & District Writers Circle which was looking for new members. I got a reply from the Secretary, Doreen Fletcher, and subsequently went to a Circle meeting as a guest.

It was a day I will never forget, for two reasons. I had never done such a brazen thing in my life, having never written more than a school essay or a long newsy letter. OK, so my father wrote books and my grandmother a social history of the "troubles" in Ireland, but that was not on my CV! The second reason is that it was a day which altered the course of the rest of my life.

I walked into the library building and picked up, in the porch, a scarab beetle which had probably fallen out of a signet ring. I'm not normally a superstitious fool, but I never found an owner for my beetle and, for good or ill, I still carry it in my purse.

Sitting round a big, library table were my fellow would-be writers and introductions were made. As I sat and listened (in some trepidation), everyone read their various pieces. They read well and I became absorbed. There was one young girl though who didn't do so well and this gave me courage as people tried to help her through and questioned her about her ideas. I learned later that she was a bit disabled and rather a trial – but at the time she seemed in the same category as myself, a bit inept. I thought to myself, "if she can do it, so can I". Doreen asked me to write a sample piece to show the Committee what I could do, and she would let me know as soon as there was a vacancy.

When I got home, a brain-wave hit me. I would write about the members as characters from Alice in Wonderland. The gathering round the table reminded me of the Mad Hatter's Tea Party. The method of determining turns to read by taking a card from the pack also seemed to fit. Luckily, the Chairman, Jeremy, who had a quirky sense of humour, liked my piece and no-one took too much exception to being called a dormouse or a mock-turtle. So I was in!

Since that day, I have had a go at many things and even had the temerity to start my own U3A circle, and make a host of new friends. Later on, I left the Farnham Circle to care for my husband in his last years, but every year I was invited back for the Christmas Lunch. Eventually, Jeremy died, some other members re-located and the Circle itself collapsed. Later, Jonathan and Pauline re-started it and one day they came to lunch here with me. Meanwhile, Jonathan's wife, Stella, had also died and Pauline's husband was gravely ill.

Somehow that lunch-party went rather well. Jonathan and I have had other Red Letter Days together, but that first one must have set the ball rolling, or the dominoes falling, or the roses being painted red, and now I'm like the Cheshire cat; all grins and whiskers. I hope I don't fade too soon!

What I see from where I stand

What I see from where I stand are two large, limp paper tapestries hanging from the rafters of the stable block in Montacute House. The actors have long since gone but these artifacts bear witness to the trouble taken in the filming of Wolf Hall.

We were not able to walk around the house as it had closed by the time we got there, so we strolled instead in the garden and the car park.

This was a very emotive place for me. I came to know it well in the late 1970's when we first came to England to live. We bought a house in Norton-sub-Hamdon, a few miles from Montacute. It turned out to have extensive dry-rot and we lost money on its sale. We were very green in those days. Nevertheless we were also happy-go-lucky and had two good years there. My husband got a job with the Yeovil Hospital gardeners to supplement my physiotherapy salary. That was how we came to be friendly with the Head Gardener at Montacute. One of "nature's gentlemen", he lived on the estate with his wife and family. We had many happy times together.

Our elder daughter got married from Norton Church and the younger one got a summer job at Montacute House, serving in the café and shop.

Now, Jonathan and I have found an enchanting B & B in the village and we often stop off there for a night on our way home from visiting family in Torquay. I still have some very good friends nearby.

We are making our own memories there.

Here is a poem I wrote on our last visit.

A walk in Montacute gardens

As sunlight slants thro' dusty air
We wander past the brooding trees.
Lavender spreads ancient scent
Over misty ground.
A church clock
Strikes the evening hour.

Paper tapestries hang limply
In the stables' musty gloom.
Forgotten knights
Resplendent in their armour;
Snort of horses, impatient still.
Actors all long gone.

We head now for the pub's bright lights,
Lure of voices and parked cars
Incongruous in the ancient Square.

Here my harboured memories
Whisper in today's hard world.

Loose living

Do not lose this hallowed page
these thoughts that you have saved.
You are not qualified to gauge their worth
so tuck them up to find again
when age has mellowed them.

Thus you counsel me.
You know my pen is profligate
my filing system out-of-date
and storage space inadequate.
Receipts make do with clothes pegs.
Finance knows its place.

Photos come and go
like taxis from the rank.
I sleep amongst my treasures.
Potions and pills, cosmetics, letters
all rub shoulders round my bed.

Christmas makes it worse,
I never used to live like this.

Augh, come give us a kiss!

A decade of continental holidays

My first holiday away with Jonathan was a disaster! We contracted the norovirus and spent Christmas together in an isolation ward in Interlaken hospital.

Nothing daunted, we set off for Rocomadour in the Dordogne on pilgrimage. We made friendships on this trip which have endured to this day. We loved the wild countryside and the chapel frescos, and felt refreshed.

A trip to Vienna followed next. We explored the Hapsburg palaces, went on the trail of "The Third Man", enjoyed the museums and galleries, including the Secession with its pictures by Egon Sheila and Gustave Klimpt. We took in a concert at the Schonbrunn Palace and "The Magic Flute" at the Opera House. It was a feast – with sachetortes!

By contrast, we went to Krakov and empathised with the Polish people, enjoyed the city university and churches and the lovely mushroom soup. We went down the salt mine at Wieliczka a quarter of a mile underground to St Kinga's chapel, a church carved out of the rock salt. The altar, statues and biblical tableaux, were topped by chandeliers which sent out an eerie glow from the sparkling salt crystals. Thankfully, we were hoisted to the surface in a miners' cage. It was an experience I would not have wanted to miss.

Later on, we took to river cruising on the Seine and Oise in a converted barge called the Anacolouthe. The crew were tireless, the food and wine delicious. On a later occasion, we undertook a cruise on the Rhone and Saone, surrounded by historic towns and lavender fields. We were on a German ship, rather too regimented for our taste but we had good company and laughed a lot.

On a subsequent trip to Normandy, we visited van Gogh's grave and "The Field of Crows".

Trips to Amsterdam and Paris were also undertaken. Another memorable journey took us to Barcelona, a favourite of Jonathan who had a Spanish grandmother who had been born there. I also harbour warm feelings for the Spanish and consider them to be very like the Irish in temperament.

This year, we decided to stay on home ground and took ourselves to the Derbyshire Peak District, staying in elegant Buxton and visiting Chatsworth House. This had been a long-standing ambition of mine, ever since poaching the Duke of Devonshire's trout in Lismore all those years ago.

Mobile phones

Sitting upstairs in a café window having coffee with my grand-daughter, looking down into the town square. . . . .

Every single person there is clutching a mobile phone. The church clock may stand at ten to three and honey be for sale on the market stall, but they are all oblivious, children now of the global family. Home is the pressure of a finger on a number, digit on digit.

"Hi ! XX U ! C U soon..."

I raise my eyes and watch the pigeons fly and settle on the statue, waiting for scraps from the stall holders as they dismantle their wares.

I am becoming cynical in my old age. My grand-daughter doesn't understand my complaint – and she is so loving that I feel chastened.

I suspect though that I'm not the only person of my generation to regret the advent of the ubiquitous mobile phone.

Time and tide wait for no man

When I was a toddler why was the tide always in?
No space for sand-castles, with flag and moat.
Away they would float.
Rock pools were swamped.
No crabs to chase or anemones to tickle
For the little pickle.

When I became a swimmer the tide was always out.
Miles out.
Having shed my clout
I'd flop across a wide, wide beach
In rubber flippers
Only to wallow in endless rows of shallow ripples.

When I wanted to picnic there were always wasps
Among the dunes.
Sand-flies on the tide-line.
Mother would forget to bring the wine.
A donkey would wander by and eat the sandwiches.
No-one would volunteer to rinse the dishes.

Now I am old and want to walk hand-in-hand
Along the sand
Watching the yachts go round the bay
A wind is blowing off the sea.
Too cold to sit
And listen to the lads' brass band.

I wonder if it's different on a Caribbean Isle
Beneath the palms
Or do coconuts drop on one's head?
Do the natives carry spears
And do Aussie beaches all have sharks?
Time could tell me.

The tide of life though may not wait.

The great sale

Call it "spring cleaning" or "life laundry" or what you will, but once a year the housewives of Petersfield go crazy. Cupboards are emptied, wardrobes depleted, curtains washed and book cases re-arranged. Cakes are baked and posters designed; for it is the time of the Great Sale!

In April, for one week, one half of the team of ladies don red aprons, adjust their spectacles, grab a pen and a sandwich, and ensconce themselves in the Festival Hall, surrounded by boxes of labels. The stage is set with rows of mirrors, the auditorium arrayed with rows of metal clothes horses and literally thousands of coat hangers. Then the other half of the ladies appear with dozens and dozens of bin bags, cardboard boxes, suit-cases and countless car-loads of "stuff"!

Finally, the labelling frenzy begins. Each article has to be labelled with a price and a letter of the alphabet. "A" means the donor wants it back if it doesn't sell for the asking price. "B" means it can be reduced in price progressively over the three days of the Sale with the donor taking half. "C" means the whole sum raised is given to the charity.

To Save the Children, in fact.

Refreshments are on sale (even light lunches these days) and all one's friends are there over the three days. No class distinctions, no false modesty. Brave husbands can be found there, mulling over the book-stalls or changing their trousers back-stage. The Great Sale saves more than the Children! The whole enterprise is simple, ingenious, tedious and, above all, effective. Every year, a total in excess of £20,000 is raised for the cause, and we all appear in each other's cast-offs for another year.

It's fun, it's damned hard work and long may it continue.

Our South Downs town

The argument is over.
Boundaries set, including Western Weald
And with it our town Petersfield.
Its Norman Church confronts the market stalls
Lavender and watercress, apple juice and sausages.

The Spain, historic Sheep Street and St Peter's Road
Sketch patterned arteries around the Market Square.
From town pubs' local brews, rough geniality
Jostles incongruously with quieter pursuits.
Here's the Physic Garden where we sit and dream
Among the herbs and ancient burgage plots.
Time was when these were tilled for hungry travellers
Resting at our stage-coach pull in on the old A3.

Heath Pond echoes to the chat of bread-crumbed ducks
While nearby hills are stippled white with sheep.
Further up on high green downland swards
Uppark nowadays resides in peace
Fresh from fiery metamorphosis.

History is seeping through the chalk
To all of us, the modern pilgrims here.

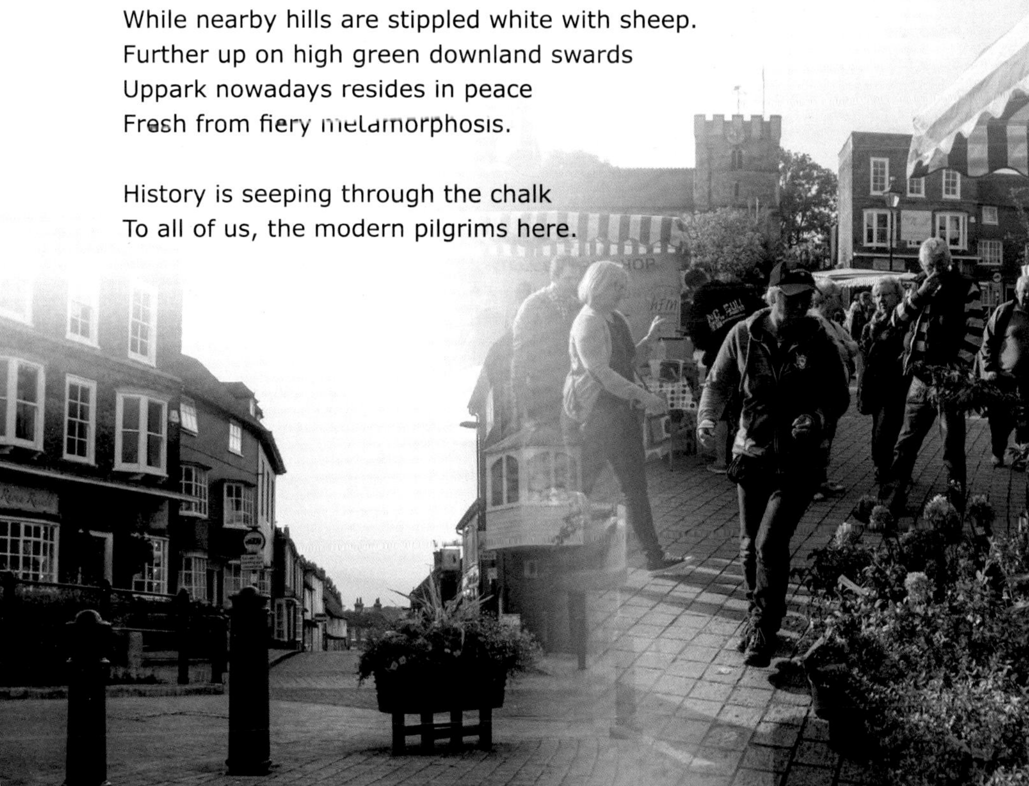

The queen bee

Gather round and watch me wiggle.
Listen to the buzzin'.
Follow me and you'll be lucky;
Flowers by the 'doz'in'.

Ripe and yellow in the fields,
Lovely golden pollen!
Fill yourselves with nature's nectar
Whilst it's for the takin'.

Days will come when you'll be hungry;
Glad of anything that's wavin'.
Come and feel the swarmin' vibes.
Now's the time for learnin'!

Help to make the golden honey
In the happy summer hives.